i

Published by Anna Nikita Media
annanikitamedia.com

Cover design & interior images by Sputnik Creative Design

Manufactured in the United States of America
Copyright 2016 by Anna Nikita

ISBN 978-0-9974550-0-7

Disclaimer: The contents of this book contain the opinions of its author, are for entertainment purposes only, and should not be considered as any form of therapy, advice, diagnosis or treatment of any kind, whether medical, mental, or spiritual. It is the reader's sole responsibility to seek expert advice, counseling, or medical treatment from professional and licensed individuals.

Errors: You are welcome to help us correct any errors, omissions, typos, etc. simply by dropping us a note at oops@annanikitamedia.com.

Seeing so many dear friends suffer heartbreak, guilt, rejection, and insecurity inflicted by divorce, inspired me to write this book.

Contents

Let's *not* split up   1
   Why is love blind?   5

Before tying the knot   9
   Jealosy   17
   How long do you wait?   19

First years of marriage   23
   Fizzle   28
   Bonding   30

Does the 7-year itch
really exist?   33
   The astrologer   34
   The biological anthropologist   36
   The psychologist   39

Your home   45
   What is feng shui?   53

Fighting is inevitable   57

Sex   69

Children   81

Stepchildren   95

Trouble in paradise   105
   Money problems and
   job loss   108
   Losing a loved one   114

It's always the season
for gifts   125
   And then there were bunnies   133

Growing older together   135

It's all in your mind   142

Tying it all together   147

Bibliography   149

Your wisdom – a place for
thoughts and life lessons you might
want to write down (and share)   153

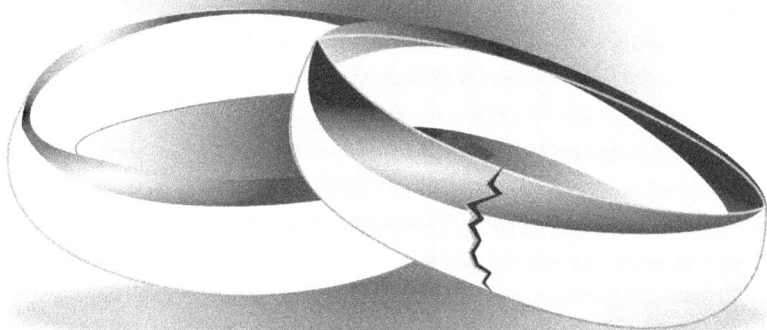

Let's *not* split up

*In the beginning there was love
and passion...*

How many break-ups and divorces do you know about? A bunch, I bet! All around us relationships are dropping like flies.

It doesn't help, of course, that divorce became socially acceptable and almost cool, thanks to media hype. Glamorous movie stars juggle a spectacular career, several kids, and look like a million bucks, while dating barely legal eye candy. It's all fluff of course, but even so, most of us can't afford a staff of nannies, chauffeurs, and housekeepers. Keeping an old fashion family together makes a lot more sense and generally results in a happier and better life.

Once the break-up happens, you enter a whirlwind. Have kids? Now you're about to do some serious juggling. The dating world is brutal. The new normal of engaging through online sites and swiping your phone silly throws your life into the mating meat grinder. Oh, you will have sex, all right, but a fulfilling and stable long-term relationship is pretty damn difficult to come by. Creating a successful household after a divorce involving kids is possible, but oh-so tough and often heartbreaking, as it can force prioritizing one loved one at the expense of another.

Before you throw it all away, sit down and take a deep breath, or two. Why did you make that commitment in the first place? There was love! There was crazy passion, romance, laughter and fun... and you were absolutely sure that it would last forever.

What happened? Life became too fast, too serious, too boring?

UN-fast it
UN-serious it
UN-boring it

Give it a chance. Having a traditional family may not be cool these days, but it is a classic. What's the definition of a classic? Judged over time, something that is generally acknowledged to be of the highest quality and outstanding example of its kind. Simple, elegant, not subject to the whims of fashion.

Do it for yourselves. Do it for your friends and family. Most importantly, do it for your kids.

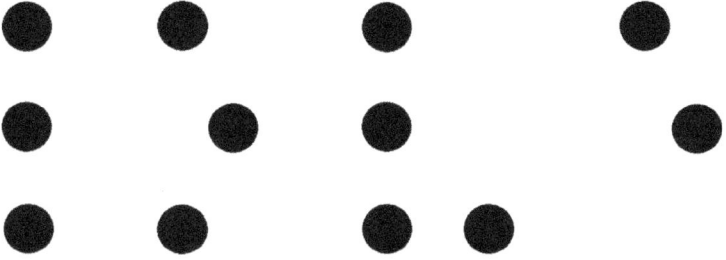

Why is love
blind?

What really happens when we fall in love? According to biological anthropologist Dr. Helen Fisher (2016), one of the preeminent "love scientists" today, when we fall deeply in love, our oldest part of the brain gets activated. That particular area is associated with drive, craving, obsession, and motivation. At the same time, the prefrontal cortex, an area of the brain that is responsible for decision-making, logic, and planning ahead, gets shut down. (Big Think, "The Science of Love")

So basically, we lose our ability to think clearly as we are consumed by this emotion. Maybe that's why love is considered to be blind all over the world.

Before tying the knot

Remember that marriage is a merger of two, often very different, families. Invest your time while dating to figure out and befriend as many members of your future spouses' family as you can. Be prepared to encounter personalities that don't fit with your own. Knowing this will help you when planning your big day and the many future holiday gatherings.

Most importantly, study the person you are planning to spend the rest of your life with.

do your HOME WORK

Do take your time.

Figure out the good and bad qualities of your future spouse. Can you live with them? Remember, we're all on our best behavior in the early stages of dating.

Go ahead and ask yourself a bunch of questions – and be truthful! Is your partner overly frugal or likes to spend too much? Loves to drink or not at all and gives you a dirty look when you're having a glass of wine? Always or never horny? Temperamental or low key? A slob or an obsessive cleaner? Night person or a crack of dawn type?

Ask tough questions.

Are you compatible in bed? How about outside the bedroom? Are you on the same wave as far as your energy levels? Couch potato or Energizer bunny? What you're willing to live with now may become a marriage breaker later. Keep in mind that people generally don't change.

Don't be pressured into committing to get married until you are 100% sure that the two of you have compatible and complementary qualities, and you are willing to live with any shortcomings.

Do

consider pre-marital counseling. **Professionals**

(or clergy, if you prefer)

are not emotionally involved, and have the training and experience to ask the right questions.

You are in love. Love is blind. Strongly recommended!

Don't
talk about previous affairs or loves. You don't have to hide the fact that you were previously married or were in a relationship, but dredging up old flames can be disastrous. Always steer away from discussing intimate details from your past.

Do
talk about whether the two of you would like to have children one day, or simply have a pet instead.

Don't
get pregnant without your partner's consent, ladies. This can be an unpleasant surprise for your partner and you might end up alone and in a mess.

Do

discuss religion, what part of your upbringing it was, and what it means to you now. Absolutely cover the subject of raising the kids in a certain religion, especially if the two of you are from different religious backgrounds.

Don't

deceive your partner by saying that you're not religious or spiritual, if you actually are.

Jealousy

It's quite normal to be possessive of somebody you absolutely adore. In fact, you should be worried if there's indifference. But, controlling your emotions is important here, as being overly jealous, if unwarranted, has to be suppressed.

Trust should be a part of a healthy relationship. There's no need to spy on each other or go through personal things.

Being paranoid about your partner's fidelity can be flattering at first, but quickly becomes tiresome and destructive.

What makes your relationship work?

"Man and woman are two different kinds of animals that end up in one cage. You can either claw each other to death or learn how to live together."

- My mom, married to my dad for 45 years

How long do you wait (before tying that knot)?

According to Dr. Helen Fisher (2016), it's a good idea to spend extensive time together before making that big decision. By doing so, you allow those intense feelings of romantic love that cloud your brain to subside a little, allowing for a more clear-headed decision. Adopt a "slow love" approach to learn as much as possible about the person you are about to wed, and whether you're a good fit together.

Dr. Fisher recommends waiting at least two years before saying "I do". There is wisdom in this, as you will experience two yearly cycles together. You'll be able to see how your future spouse handles holidays and birthdays, extended families and friends, vacations, and those times when you're under the weather. Not to worry, according to Dr. Fisher, you both will still be able to sustain that intense feeling of romantic love within this time. ("The Science of Love", *Big Think*)

First years of
marriage

Darlings, it's a marathon, not a sprint.

The first few years of marriage are critical. It will take a lot of **compromise** and **creativity** to keep it together. When times are tough, recite your marriage vows again. You'll be fine - patience, **patience**.

Do

be patient! As you settle into a routine, things get less intense. Remember to "throw a log in the fire" now and then by doing something you used to do when the two of you were still dating. Maybe a romantic picnic in the park, or something naughty.

Don't

be a bore. Be open-minded to your partner's suggestions. Rule of thumb: "I'll try it at least once, if it's safe."

Do

watch each other's back. Never take sides with anyone else, even if your spouse is wrong. Hash things out privately, if you feel it is needed.

You have to think and act like one unit now. When your husband/wife sees that kind of loyalty it will be highly appreciated and rewarded.

Don't

gossip about your partner. Don't discuss your intimate life with anyone (even your mother or best friend).

Do find common interests and hobbies that can be carried throughout your long marriage, such as music, hiking, photography, bicycling, cooking, etc. Reading something funny to each other at bedtime once in while is great for your bonding.

play together = stay together

Don't go on separate vacations. It may seem like you are giving each other space, but in reality it will only create separate memories.

Do enjoy each other for a while (a couple of years) before having babies, unless you're older, and running out of time.

Don't seek advice from your friends or relatives when to have a child. This is only for you two to decide.

Fizzle

Unlike the typical Hollywood scripts, growing apart doesn't necessarily happen with some earth-shattering event like infidelity, or a heated drama involving door slamming arguments and flying dishes.

Most relationships end with a whimper rather than a bang. The process of growing apart develops over a pretty long period of time, like a creeping cancer. Lack of affection, sexless months, and loss of interest in your partner's life all slowly destroy the relationship. Devoting yourself blindly to the kids at the expense of your spouse is one of the most common causes of growing apart.

And so **one day you're** eating dinner together, and **sitting across from a total stranger** with absolutely nothing in common and nothing to talk about.

Bonding

Creating a bond that goes beyond love and passion is essential. Spend as much time together as possible - this will help you become best friends and partners. It means saying "Sorry, I can't hang out today" to your friends at times. This might upset them, but you're married now.

Does the 7-year itch really exist?

3 theories:

The Astrologer

There are theories suggesting that our bodies and minds develop and change every seven years. Austrian philosopher and educator Rudolf Steiner, a supremely prolific writer who penned over 330 **volumes** of works, and known popularly as the founder of biodynamic agriculture, (a holistic approach to farming, whereby the farm is treated as one integrated organism that thrives without synthetic fertilizers, and responds to cycles of the wider cosmos.) Today, this system is used by thousands of farmers throughout the world – just go to your nearby organic farmers market and ask a few of them.

Well, Dr. Steiner had a take on our development too. According to him, we are all going through 7-year cycles that are mystically connected with one of the solar system planets. Every seven years our personal affiliation with a particular planet shifts to a different one and we experience profound evolutions in our consciousness and physical changes to our bodies. (www. rudolfsteinerweb.com)

These important changes in personal growth, experience, knowledge and goals every seven years can make a marriage less stable and increase the probability of conflict and even divorce.

The Biological Anthropologist

Dr. Helen Fisher (2015), the scientist who advises us to wait 2 years before getting married, has a different take on it. According to her extensive research, we still maintain certain ancient reproductive patterns that influence our lives and decision-making. It is a known fact that the more advanced hunter-gatherer societies tended to birth children roughly four years apart. Her premise is that children become more self-sufficient at that age and can be successfully cared for, even (my assumption) by the extended community.

This pattern leads Dr. Fisher to hypothesize that the four year cycle would allow unhappy couples to split up and produce offspring with others, while at the same time not endangering their mutual child's welfare.

Our present-day four-year divorce spike phenomenon may well be a remnant of that "ancestral reproductive strategy" to stay together just long enough to raise the child through its very early years. As a result, we might be susceptible to a "natural weak point" in our relationships that surfaces after four years.

The hope is that by understanding our human hardwiring a bit better, we can anticipate, and take the necessary precautions to avoid a catastrophic split. ("Is There a Biological Basis for the 7-Year Itch?" *Scientific American*)

The Psychologist

Dr. Larry A. Kurdek (1999), a psychology professor from Wright State University conducted a marital happiness study by asking over 500 couples a set of questions every year over their first ten years of marriage (by the last year only 93 responded).

As expected, the first several years produced answers that reflected a high satisfaction and happiness rate. But as time went by the answers reflected that the "levels of marital quality" tended to trend downwards. Couples with children (not stepchildren) experienced a more rapid decline in their marital quality.

The key finding was that there were two distinct periods of time where the quality decreased rapidly – first, during the first four years, which corroborates Dr. Fisher's findings (our biological anthropologist), and again after the seventh year, mirroring both the commonly held belief and Dr. Steiner's astrologically based one. Interestingly, both husbands and wives reported similar declines within these timeframes.

Dr. Kurdek explains the first dip as an almost inevitable result of the marriage starting from such a high point that it has nowhere to go but down. Basically, we tend to overlook those irritating little things that our partner does early in the relationship, like leaving his coffee mug by the computer AGAIN. As time goes by, however, we tend to develop a shorter fuse for these things.

His take on the second dip – the 7-year one is that we might tend to succumb to boredom and the daily grind of our relationship. We know everything about our partner and life must be better and more exciting on the outside. (Vol 35(5) 1283-1296, *Developmental Psychology*)

Well, there you have it...

I have no idea whether this so-called "itch" is the result of astrology, boredom, or mating behavior, but it definitely seems to play a role in our love lives. In my opinion, there is no magic number when it comes to maintaining a happy relationship. The studies do seem to agree that couples need to put in the extra effort every day to sustain happy marriages. If a couple doesn't keep investing in their relationship, the marriage will fall apart - no matter how long they've been together.

It seems to be pretty difficult to apply any scientific reasoning as to why some marriages make it and some fail. I feel that there are so many factors that come into play: maturity, ability to communicate and compromise, moral compass, and simply, love.

Your home

"Home is where you feel at home and are treated well."
- Dalai Lama

"Decorate your home. It gives the illusion that your life is more interesting than it really is."
- Charles M. Schulz

"Home is any four walls that enclose the right person"
- Helen Rowland

Do

keep your home clean, organized, and efficient.

Don't

spend all your time cleaning. Remember - housework kills!

Do

keep your bedroom beautiful and inviting. Make up your bed every morning.

Don't

bring guests for a tour of your bedroom. Protect your privacy. Don't jinx your sex life.

Do

move things, furniture, pictures, and memorabilia around to **keep** things fresh and new energy flowing throughout your home.

Don't

hang pictures or photos of deceased or divorced people in your home, or anything that might bring out bad or negative memories.

Do insist on having a sit-down dinner with your whole family a couple of times a week. Make sure that everybody participates in the conversation. It's a good idea to encourage your kids to come to the table prepared to share some interesting fact or event that you can all then discuss while having a meal together.

Don't

allow electronics at the dinner table.

Make a pact that if you're eating together, all phones are turned OFF, including yours. A media-free time ensures a meaningful family time.

What makes your relationship work?

"We always have dinner together. I don't care if I eat at 10 PM. I always wait up for him. If he's grumpy, I make sure to find out why. We would tell or text each other a few times a day that we love each other."

- Danny and Marco, together for 12 years

Do

make sure your young kids have a play area. Have designated toy bins to keep things contained.

Don't

let your home resemble a Toys "R" Us store. Remember that adults live here too.

What is
Feng Shui?

There is no great mystery to understanding feng shui. It is simply about correct energy flow. Meaning "wind-water", feng shui is the philosophy of creating harmony within our surroundings.

This ancient Chinese wisdom provides guidance to strengthen positive energy and create beauty in the process. Following its practical advice allows you to transform your home into a true sanctuary - a place where you feel healthy, happy, and motivated.

Whether you have a small apartment or a large house, if it's arranged wisely it will bring you joy, creativity, and good sexual energy. Keep your home clutter free and keep negative and jealous people away.

Your home should be your castle

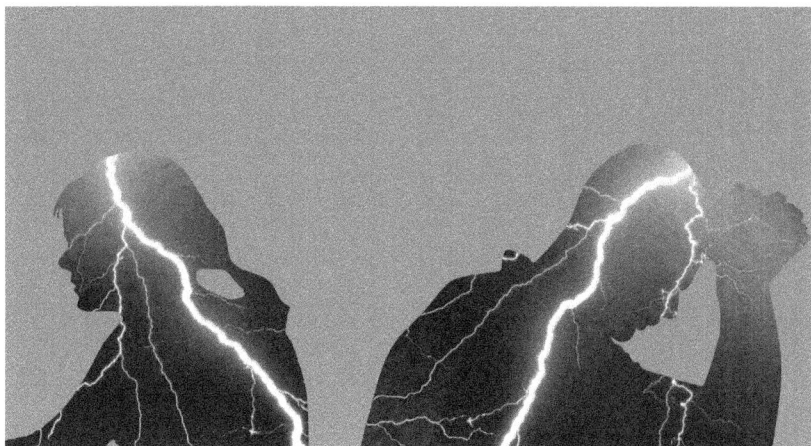

Fighting is inevitable

*Even the most perfect and
adorable couples fight.*

Keep one thing in mind **when** you are **going to war** with your other half - **your goal is to stay together forever**, not to prove that you are right. This will put things in to perspective for you. Try to avoid confrontations without giving it the proper thought and remember the old "count to ten" advice.

Definitely avoid alcohol before discussing the issue. It will prevent clear thinking and can turn ugly and cause permanent damage to both body and soul.

Women are known for having a very, very long memory, and can bring up a slight or dig up an old problem from 10 years ago on demand.

Men absolutely hate this trait because it takes them aback and muddies the situation. There's no real benefit in it for either party. It will just make your fight longer and more complicated. Try to keep it down to business and get it over as quickly as possible. Remember, any good resolution will involve a compromise by both sides.

Do

keep your fights short and to the point. Work toward a compromise, then quickly kiss and make up. Life is too short to be pissed off.

Don't

bring it up again once the fight is done. When its over, its over - just let go no matter what.

As strange as it sounds... it's a good idea...

Do bring up a good quality in your

partner during a fight – as long as it's sincere, and doesn't sound sarcastic.

For example, "You're a very smart person and I respect your opinion..." or "You're a fantastic mother (father), husband (wife)..." Use this to help diffuse the situation and introduce a positive statement; however, never add a "but" and a negative statement after that.

Don't

say something that will cause long-term damage to your relationship during the heat of the battle. Never belittle your mutual sex life, or your partner's performance in bed.

Keep the in-laws and your opinions about them out of the fight.

Do

establish a working relationship with your partner's side of the family. Study their family dynamics to figure out why your spouse has certain inclinations and tendencies. It will give you a good idea how to deal with them during conflict.

Don't

complain about your significant other to your mom or dad. Grow up - you're married now.

Do always sleep together in the same bed, even after the fight

of the century. Hold hands or make toe contact even if you are still angry at each other.

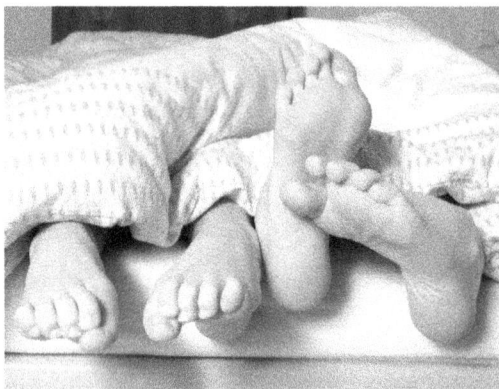

Don't bring your bad mood and the big fight into the bedroom.

Make a rule that it will not be considered defeatist. Establish a pact beforehand how you will both deal with this. For instance, you agree that once past the bedroom door you both count to three together and hug.

Do resolve an issue if it is really bothering you.

In order to avoid a fight, leave a handwritten note, NOT an email or text.

"My dearest! I adore you. However, your stinky socks are in my sink again, and giving me nightmares. Please! Your Pumpkin."

Don't lose your sense of humor.

Some fights are just plain stupid. Turn it into a joke and be done with it.

Stinky socks? Blah, blah... May that be the biggest problem in your marriage.

What makes your relationship work?

"Fight fair."

- Ronda has been married to Ali for 25 years

Sex

We humans are physical creatures, so it's very important to maintain mutual sexual desire for as long as possible. It's not easy though, because by definition "long term" means that you both will go through several body transformations throughout your marriage such as pregnancy, weight loss, weight gain, and even injury. And don't forget those inevitable wrinkles and stretch marks.

Being cognizant about **protecting your sexuality is very important**. It goes for both guys and gals. Yes! We girls need to look yummy for you, but we also need to desire you, in order to seduce you. The point is - **keeping your partner interested in you sexually for a long-long-long time is an art!**

Do look good and groomed for each other. Always be ready for romance.

Don't forget the following:

No
"no shave November"

No
sleeping in an old stained T-shirt

No
jungle "down under"

No
toenails that scrape the floor

Do create time for sex.

Even if both of you have to put it on a calendar. It is challenging when you have little ones at home. Ask a relative or a friend to take them for ice cream or a walk in the park, and hop in the shower together.

Don't make excuses!

Sex is good for your health, overall mood, and your mutual bond. You can deal with a lot of crap in life if you're sexually satisfied.

Do

have pleasant music available as well as erotic things in your bedroom.

Don't

watch anything on TV or online in the bedroom that would make you or your spouse upset or aggressive in a negative way.

Do always wear cozy, comfy, clean and inviting house garments.

Don't do anything disgusting in front of your lover. That includes, flatulence, picking your nose, ears, zits, or other forgettable images. This is not attractive or sexy.

Do get ready for sex or a romantic time with your partner the same way, as if you were going out to a fancy restaurant. Shower, shave, and smell good. It will put you in the right mood, just as getting ready to go eat gives you an appetite.

Don't criticize your partner's performance in bed under any circumstances. If one of you is getting out of shape, invest in bicycles or start taking daily walks.

Touch is very important. Make sure to connect several times a day by hugging, rubbing each other's shoulders, clasping hands, and the like.

Don't ignore each other's presence. Make sure to make eye contact often and say a few kind words to each other, even if you're just passing each other in the hallway. **Make it a habit of saying 5 nice things to your partner every day.**

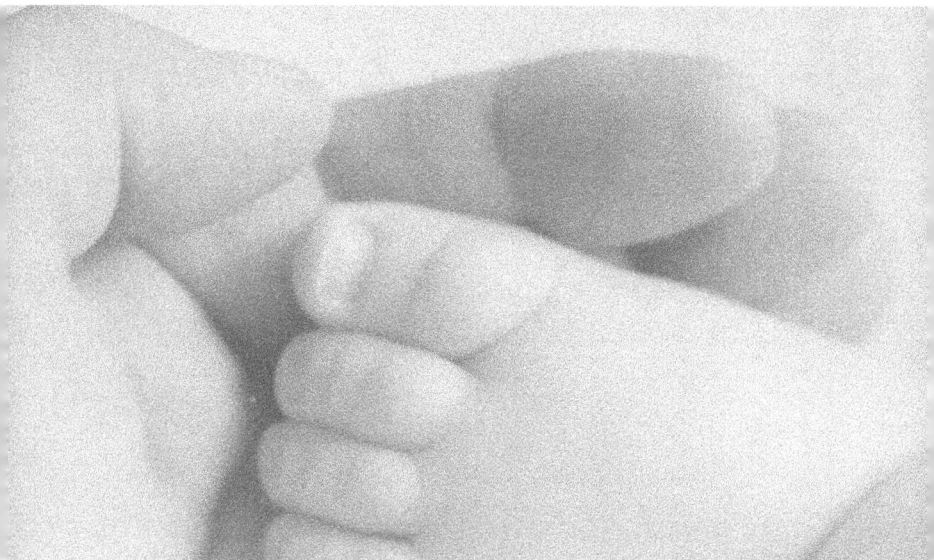

Children

The decision to have a child is a life-changing one.

You'd better be sure that you're ready: it's like putting a tattoo on your face – it's permanent! This decision will impact you and your spouse not simply until the child turns 18, but for the rest of your lives.

Ask yourself some tough questions, and above all else, be truthful.

- Are both of you emotionally ready to share your partner with another (very demanding) being?
- Can the two of you support a bigger family?
- Are you ready to give up most of your freedom to travel, sleep in on weekends, and stay up late?
- Are you ready to worry about this new person's well being for the rest of your life?

If you BOTH answered "yes" to these questions, then you're probably ready.

Do

plan to deliver the baby together. Guys don't miss the most miraculous event of your life! It's beautiful and natural. Afraid of fainting? No worries – you're already in the hospital.

Don't

make the birth of your child a social event.

There's always a comfortable couch and beverages in the waiting room for your mom, best friends, and assorted family members. Keep it authentic. It took the two of you to create a baby; it should be just the two of you to first welcome your child into this world.

Do

go on regular dates, even (or should I say, especially) if you have young kids.

Make sure that you remain boyfriend and girlfriend.

Don't allow your kids to sleep in your bedroom,

unless they're very sick and you have to keep an eye on them 24/7, or occasionally, if your spouse is out of town.

Children in your bedroom will prevent spontaneous romance, and will make one or both partners feel sexually deprived.

Do

get on the same page about disciplining your kids. Go over the rules together, and stick to them.

Don't

give in to your kids if your spouse already said "no" to something. If you feel your little angel is playing the two of you off against each other, stop everything and contact your spouse to confirm that you are both in agreement on the issue. Your child needs to know that you're a team and cannot be manipulated. And believe me, this will happen.

Do make sure to spend quality time as a family unit. Bicycle rides, playing in the park, hiking, camping - these activities will make your family stronger and create beautiful memories together for the rest of your lives.

Remember again: families that play together stay together.

Don't postpone simple trips while you wait to make money, and take your family on that extravagant vacation. Kids grow up really fast. Enjoy each other and create wonderful memories by going on many quality, but inexpensive, outings.

Trips to the museum or art and science exhibitions elevate us and take us away from our everyday grind. It's a wonderful thing to do with your kids, teaching them early on about the fine arts and cultures from around the world, as well as the wonders of our universe.

It's up to you to make those times exciting and pleasant for them. It's a common misconception that art is boring. My husband and I play a game that keeps the whole family engaged. Each person has to find five favorite artworks and take a photo of them. During lunch or dinner everyone shares what he or she found and explains why each was chosen. It becomes almost like a treasure hunt.

What makes your relationship work?

"Taking romantic trips without the kids on a regular basis. We try to do this every other trip."

- Sergei, married forever to Anna Nikita

Do volunteer in your children's class.

It's a wonderful way to participate in their school life and make them proud that you're involved.

This extra effort will lead to more secure children and provide reassurance that you truly care.

Don't embarrass your kids by trying to fit in, and acting like

you are their age when their peers are present.

Be respectful of their space when they're with their friends or at school. Don't publicly baby them or tell potentially embarrassing stories from their past.

Do let your kids be kids.

It's OK if they get dirty from playing outside, or come home with knee holes in their pants or tights – they will eventually grow out of this and you won't have to visit Target every other week.

Don't expect your child to always be that picture-perfect image you see in magazines.

Buy expensive clothes only for special occasions (but once you do, don't forget to have them wear them whenever appropriate, as they outgrow everything fast!) **Practical and inexpensive clothing is perfect for active children** and results in less stress for you.

Mommy and me

My mom always told me that most of the fights she had with my dad were because of my brother and me. It is very difficult to disengage emotionally and do the right thing; because of the strong love we have for our kids, and the fact that they are so cute!

Mom often feels like the father is overdoing it or overreacting while disciplining one of the kids, and her instinct is to protect her child. It's part of nature.

This can cause significant tension between husband and wife. It helps to have daily communication about your kids. Talk about their grades, activities, and friends. There should be no surprises. It is hard to keep a tight family unit unless your children know that you and your spouse are a team and in charge. This is the only way you can maintain a healthy family and not lose each other in the process.

Stepchildren

You must have unconditional love for your partner to enter into a union that includes stepchildren. Don't fool yourself, it's always complicated. Even if it looks simple and everybody in the beginning acts civilized, there will be moments of resentment, manipulation, and even hatred.

The best advice I can give you is to always take the high road with your step kids, your spouse, and the ex. This is a no-win situation for you, so maintaining a sense of normal is essential. These kids are already traumatized enough by divorce or loss of a parent. Your job is not an easy one. It is wise to become a tower of strength, stability, and above all, kindness.

Do be kind, nice and diplomatic with your stepkids.

Don't allow them to be rude with you or dismissive.

Do

establish a personal relationship with your stepkids. Make sure they can always talk to you. Demonstrate that you can keep secrets.

CONFIDENTIAL

Don't inform people in front of your stepchildren that they are not biologically yours. It will damage your bond. In fact, your family's dynamics are nobody's business.

Do

Include your **stepchildren** in the family life. They **should always be welcome.** Invite them to special occasions, holidays, and vacations. Stay in touch.

Don't

Spank or hit your stepchildren, even if there was some serious wrongdoing. They will hold a grudge forever.

Instead, coordinate with your spouse, as the natural parent, to always take the lead in the discipline department.

It is extremely difficult to raise your own children. Having a functional and harmonious household with stepkids is even harder and deserves a huge amount of respect.

Keep in mind that they will be in your life forever. It's a common mistake to think that they will leave the house at 18, never to be seen or heard from again. The wisest thing you, as a stepparent, can do is to establish a healthy relationship of mutual respect with your stepchild.

It may take a few years for you to see any results of your kindness and effort. Cultivate your garden and you will be rewarded with a devoted friend for life.

Trouble in
paradise

One day your marriage will be tested. Hopefully, by that time you will have accumulated enough love, patience, and wisdom to deal with it in the proper way and protect your harmony as much as possible.

Losing a loved one, a job, or money troubles can knock you off your feet for a very long time. Your marriage can become jeopardized. The two of you will need to work together to keep things in their proper perspective and together decide what's the right thing to do in that situation.

It's OK to talk about possible scenarios before they happen, and discuss hypothetically how you would deal with them, prioritizing your health, love, and of course, the wellbeing of your children.

What makes your relationship work?

"Many people feel like marriage is the conclusion of their relationship, and they don't want to work at it anymore. A good marriage needs constant work, like tending your garden."

- Larry, married for 28 years

Money problems
and job loss

Money issues are considered to be one of the biggest triggers for divorce. It's ironic then, that we often hear the cliché that "money isn't everything" or "money can't buy you happiness."

Keeping it together while knee-deep in a financial crisis will take a lot of willpower and planning. Buckle up and make sure to keep your love life separate from your financial life. Easier said than done - I know.

Some day you will look at this time in the rear view mirror and be very proud of yourselves for pulling through together.

Do try to save for a rainy day.

Agree with your partner that you would jointly use these stashed funds only in the event of a family member getting sick in another state, an earthquake, a car accident, etc. It is wise to have a "piggy bank" that will under no circumstances be used for a pair of shoes or a phone upgrade.

Don't ever hide money from your spouse.

It's always discovered and is not only embarrassing, but also affects the level of trust, thereby compromising the very core of your bond.

Do be honest with your spouse if you lose your job or money, for whatever reason. Have a constructive conversation about dealing with the bills and budgeting going forward.

Don't conceal the seriousness of your situation

and have your partner keep spending money as usual, only to feel guilty or stupid about it later.

Do

Make sure to set up a realistic budget for your partner's extra needs if you are the primary provider, and start having money problems. This way your loved one doesn't feel "up in the air" and not included in the situation.

Don't

borrow money without telling your spouse. Two heads are better than one and the obligation will be felt by both of you.

Losing a loved one

This is a very difficult subject. Though death is an inevitable part of our lives, we take it very individually. Self-preservation doesn't allow us to feel that depth of sorrow for people who just lost somebody very dear.

Helping your spouse to deal with the grief of losing a parent or a friend can "make or break" your marriage, as it demonstrates your character, and compassion.

Losing a child (and I do not wish this on my worst enemy) is the absolute worst thing in life. It can cement your marriage or shatter it like a crystal glass.

Do

be there for your spouse even if you don't know the person who died. Remember, it takes at least a year to start feeling somewhat normal after losing someone very important in your life.

Don't

under any circumstances, say, "snap out of it", or 'it's about time to let it go", or "you haven't even seen that person in a long time".

Any **impatience** or **negativity will** cause you to **be seen as** being coarse and **insensitive**... and a disappointment.

Compassion

Compassion

Compassion

Do

create a calendar of important dates related to the deceased, such as a birthday, day of death, and holidays celebrated together. Bring the person up on those days with your partner to show you care.

Better yet, go out together that day. Have a toast **celebrating the deceased's life** or dedicate a walk or even name a trail after that special someone, who left a mark in your lover's life. Do that, and you will see how much you will be appreciated.

Don't

ignore your spouse's sadness and grief. It will pass quicker if you address it. Help your partner by talking about it. Anger and frustration is normal. Don't take anything personally.

Do

seek help. There is no wisdom in becoming a recluse and bleeding to death.

- see a doctor or specialist

- join a bereavement group

- talk to a spiritual person, or someone at your place of prayer

- find a good yoga studio.

Don't expect sorrow to disappear by itself. Ignoring the suffering and pain will bring tension and distrust and resentment into your marriage.

Do take a trip together. Remember the chapter where the need to sock away "rainy day" money was suggested? This would be it. A change of scenery can be very therapeutic.

Don't allow anybody, even family members, to hurt your partner's feelings. Protect you spouse from negative and malicious "friends", who will pry, ask inappropriate questions, and dig into the wound.

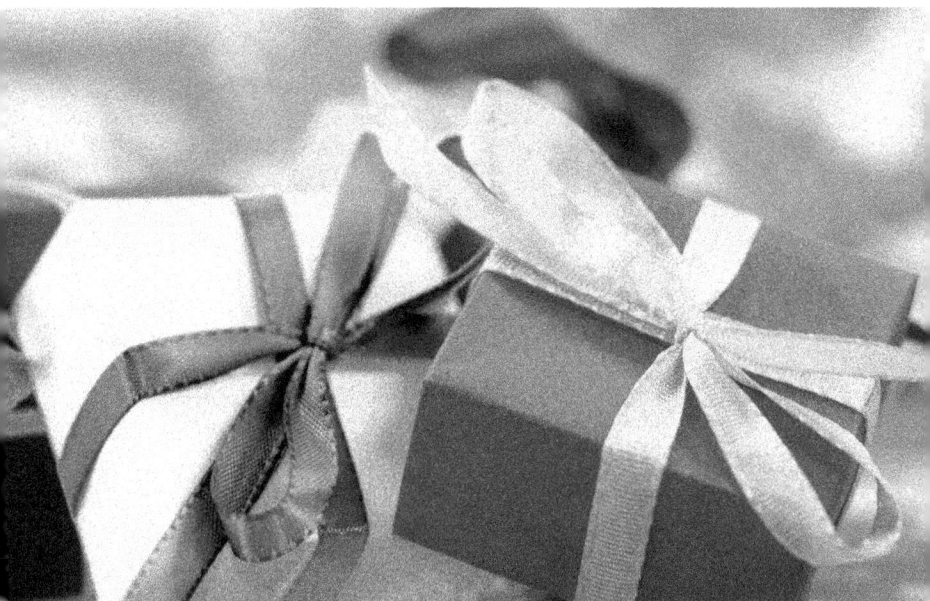

It's always the
season for gifts

"A wise lover values not so much the gift of the lover as the love of the giver."

- Thomas à Kempis, The Imitation of Christ

After a couple lives together for a good time, they pretty much already have everything they need. It doesn't mean however that you shouldn't give each other gifts. It can be something silly, like a seashell, or a lovely bottle of wine that you two will share later in the day. The point of it is that you have to remind each other regularly that you still care and love one another.

Do

make sure to **spoil each other** with little tokens of affection such as cute love notes, flowers, favorite foods, or whatever your partner's interests and desires are.

Don't

limit gift giving to just special occasions.

Do make a big deal out of your partner's

birthday, or your wedding anniversary. Give romantic gifts to each other.

Don't give practical gifts on special occasions, like

birthdays or anniversaries, such as cookware. Rule of thumb: nothing with an electrical cord, a handle, or an instruction manual.

Do

be grateful and gracious when you get any gift, be that a simple love note or an extravagance such as a new car.

Love You ♡

Don't

Be rude or sarcastic if you get a gift that you don't like, or if you didn't get the gift you wanted. It is a huge turnoff, and will make your partner nervous the next gift giving time.

It is very important to give flowers on a regular basis. It is very important to expect flowers on a regular basis. They don't have to be expensive or fancy. Wild ones are even more fabulous.

Flowers are associated with the important things in our lives: happiness, light, nature, good emotions, renewal, hope, and romance. **Having flowers around in your home** will remind you about your love, appreciation for each other, and **will start your day off with a smile**.

And then there were bunnies...

A couple in Pasadena, California pledged to give each other a bunny gift every single day of their marriage. Since 1993, this endearing expression of love created the world's largest and a bit bizarre collection, which was eventually transformed into The Bunny Museum. More than 33,000 (and growing daily) bunny toys and rabbit-related novelties can be seen in this "Hoppiest Place on Earth".

Growing older together

"In the end, it's not the years in your life that count. It's the life in your years."

- Abraham Lincoln

"Do not go gentle into that good night,
Old age should burn and rave at close of day;
Rage, rage against the dying of the light."

- Dylan Thomas

"If you live to be a hundred, I want to live to be a hundred minus one day so I never have to live without you."

- Joan Powers, Pooh's Little Instruction Book

Do stay intimate.

Physical contact is all-important. Hold hands, play footsies during dinner, hug, hug, hug.

Don't stop cuddling.

It is a very important part of your bond. Make sure to sleep together in the same bed.

Do stay fit together.

The longer you take care of yourselves – the longer you will enjoy your life, the outdoors, sex, your children, and your money.

Don't make excuses not to

have sex. It's good for you, even if you're a bit under the weather. It will do miracles for your mood, relationship, and overall health.

Do

laugh out loud **together**. It is a proven fact that people who laugh often, live longer. Enjoy life.

Don't say that you're old now, and getting older, and older, and older... yawn. Complaining about your aches and pains does not make them magically disappear, and does not make for good conversation.

Do be interested in each other's life.

Every day stay in touch and together by talking about new plans for the day, well-being issues and any concerns. It's always nice to bring something positive to the conversation, especially if one of you is down.

Don't grow apart by not being interested in one another.

After your children are out of the house it's easy to disconnect, and head in different directions. Take this time of your life to get to know each other even better.

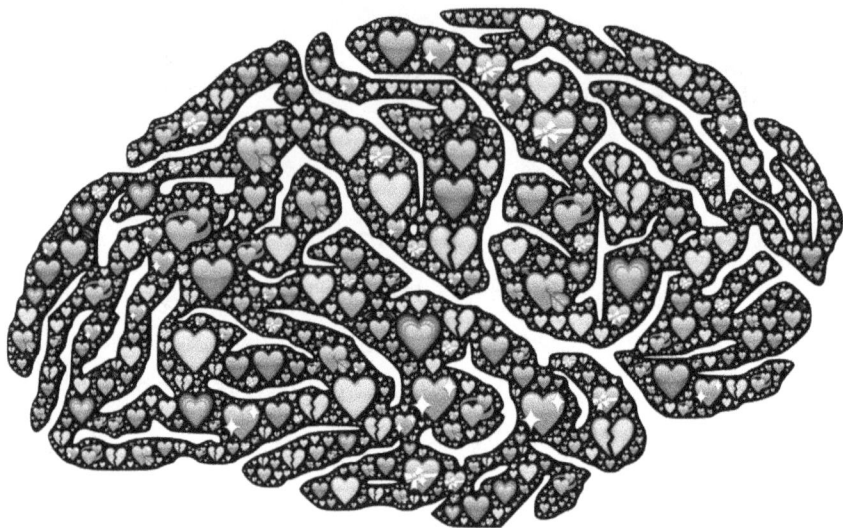

It's all in your mind

A brain scanning study (Fisher, 2008) of couples that had been married for over 21 years, and were still madly in love concluded that these happy couples showed increased activity in three brain regions linked to:

- empathy
- controlling your own emotions
- positive illusions

Ignoring what you don't like in your partner and concentrating on what you like is one of the essential recipes for a long-term relationship. It is very important to say a few nice things to your spouse several times a day. It's miraculous, and medicinal. Dr. Fisher has found evidence that doing this will reduce both cholesterol and cortisol (a stress hormone) in your partner, and boost the immune system in both of you. (Poster Session, #297, *Society for Neuroscience*)

Being in love is healthy for us.

Be with a guy who ruins your LIPSTICK not your MASCARA.

This hangs in my laundry room where I tend to spend more time than I care to.

Tying it all together

There are moments when a break-up seems like a good solution for a tough or complicated situation. Sooner or later, every couple goes through this time, thinking that a separation will be an improvement in the quality of their individual lives.

Watching so many dear friends going through the pain, suffering, rejection, and insecurity inflicted by divorce, inspired me to write this book. I hope the humble advice it contains will empower couples to take a closer look at why they got together in the first place, and energize them to fight for something so beautiful and sacred as their love and commitment to each other.

Anna Nikita

Bibliography

Big Think. February 13, 2016. The Science of Love, with Dr. Helen Fisher.
Retrieved from
https://www.youtube.com/watch?v=0YP4n9G0qtQ&feature=youtu.be

"Is There a Biological Basis for the 7-Year Itch?" (January 1, 2015) *Scientific American*
Retrieved on April 5, 2016 from
http://www.scientificamerican.com/article/is-there-a-biological-basis-for-the-7-year-itch/

Dr. Fisher's website:
http://www.helenfisher.com

Armstrong, Thomas. (August 7, 2012) "The Stages of Life According to Rudolf Steiner." *American Institute for Learning and Human Development.*
Retrieved on March 26, 2016 from
http://institute4learning.com/blog/2012/08/07/the-stages-of-life-according-to-rudolf-steiner/

"Who Was Rudolf Steiner?" *Biodynamic Association*
Retrieved on March 26, 2016 from
https://www.biodynamics.com/steiner.html

Rudolf Steiner website:
http://www.rudolfsteinerweb.com

Berger, Alisha. (October 5, 1999) "Study Finds a 7-Year Itch and a 4-Year One" *The New York Times (Health)* Retrieved on March 26, 2016 from http://www.nytimes.com/1999/10/05/health/study-finds-a-7-year-itch-and-a-4-year-one.html

Kurdek, Lawrence A. (September 1999) "The nature and predictors of the trajectory of change in marital quality for husbands and wives over the first 10 years of marriage" *Developmental Psychology, Vol 35(5) 1283-1296*

Aceveda, B, A Aron, H Fisher and LL Brown (November 2008) Poster Session #297, *Society for Neuroscience,* annual meeting

Anna Nikita is available for speaking engagements. Please contact her at:

anna@annanikitamedia.com

or visit her website at:

annanikitamedia.com

Your wisdom

a place for thoughts and life lessons
you might want to write down
(and share)

Share your wisdom:
wisdom@annanikitamedia.com
We hope to publish a follow-up volume with
our readers' helpful thoughts, so send them
in and we'll give you credit for them.